Stewart Henderson is a poet, ~~~~~~~~~~~~~
Times has described his cr~~~~~~~~~~~~~
Widely anthologised throug~~~~~~~~~~~ ~~iversity Press,
Scholastic, Bloomsbury, A&C Black and others, Stewart's verse
is set for both GCSE and Key Stage 2 in primary schools in the
UK, and their equivalent on the Republic of Ireland curriculum.
His bestselling *Who Left Grandad at the Chip Shop?* was shortlisted
for the Scottish Children's Book Awards, and *All Things Weird and
Wonderful*, alongside his various collections for adults, has seen him
become a festival favourite at such premier literary events as the
Edinburgh Book Festival, Birmingham's Young Readers UK, The
Northern Children's Book Festival and the Wigtown Book Festival.

As a regular broadcaster on BBC Radio 4, Stewart has presented
Questions, Questions for the last nine years. His programme 'The
Holy Fire', made on location in Israel, won the Jerusalem Radio
Award for Best Feature in 2006. Stewart has also presented and
contributed to some of Radio 4's 'crown jewels' such as *From Our
Own Correspondent*, *Pick of the Week*, *Broadcasting House*, *Something
Understood*, *Saturday Live* and *PM*.

Barnabas in Schools

Text copyright © Stewart Henderson 2012

The author asserts the moral right
to be identified as the author of this work

Published by
The Bible Reading Fellowship
15 The Chambers, Vineyard
Abingdon OX14 3FE
United Kingdom
Tel: +44 (0)1865 319700
Email: enquiries@brf.org.uk
Website: www.brf.org.uk
BRF is a Registered Charity

ISBN 978 1 84101 893 5

First published 2012
Reprinted 2012
10 9 8 7 6 5 4 3 2 1

All rights reserved

Acknowledgments
The poem 'I take me for granted' was commissioned by BBC Radio 4 for the series 'Wide
Awake at Bedtime', first broadcast January 2008, with the programme(s) being subsequently
repeated.

A catalogue record for this book is available from the British Library

Printed and bound by CPI Group (UK) Ltd, Croydon, CR0 4YY

Tony Street
October 2014

Poetry Emotion

50 original poems to spark an imaginative approach to topical values

Stewart Henderson

By the same author

Poetry: *Carved into a Scan*; *Whose Idea of Fun is a Nightmare?*; *Fan Male*; *Assembled in Britain*; *A Giant's Scrapbook*; *Homeland*; *Limited Edition*; *Still, Facing Autumn*

Poetry for children: *Who Left Grandad at the Chipshop?*; *All Things Weird and Wonderful*

General: *Greenbelt: Since the beginning*; *Adrift in the Eighties: The Strait Interviews* (ed.)

* For Flossie, Rosie and Emily *

Acknowledgments

I'd like to thank the numerous assorted staff (as well as the pupils) of so many schools throughout the UK, whose steadfast dedication and commitment have ensured that my time at their schools has been challenging and inspiring—in particular, the head teacher, staff and children at Royston Primary School, Glasgow, for their deep teaching about 'letting go of our balloons'. Many of the poems in this book have been directly and indirectly inspired by Royston School and its courageous response to community trauma. In conjunction with that, I'd like to take the opportunity to thank musician and songwriter Stephen Fischbacher for his enabling and tremendous work in schools, and for his encouragement of children towards emotional literacy through his songs and performances.

A very special thanks to my commissioning editor, Sue Doggett, for setting *Poetry Emotion* in motion. I have so valued her sensitive guidance and belief.

*

Contents

It's not fair!

General themes

Getting on and falling out

Going for goals!

New beginnings

Saying 'no' to bullying

Good to be me

Changes

Emotional skills

Self-awareness

Managing feelings

Motivation

Social skills

*

Foreword

Poetry speaks in as many voices as there are people to read it, conveying everything from complex ideas to simple truths. The wonderful thing about Stewart Henderson's kind of writing is that he always manages to cover both at once.

The first time I heard him perform his own poetry, in 1996, was unforgettable. I was so bowled over, I immediately asked him to write regularly for the television worship programme on which I was, at that time, Series Producer for BBC1. I had been looking for a long time for someone who could speak to a general audience, of all faiths and none, about beliefs, spiritual expression and the joys and sorrows of some of life's most profound experiences, in a way that had the capacity to engage naturally and touch deeply.

Stewart knew exactly where to start and, with consummate skill and the unmistakable voice of authenticity, he took the audience on a very special journey. This collection of poems has, I believe, the same quality of travel. I read them, delighted but not surprised by their range and honesty. I could picture him in my mind's eye at one of his regular visits to the Greenbelt festival, holding a roomful of children spellbound, making them gasp with anticipation or having them squeal and laugh in a magical connection with young hearts and minds. He makes it look effortless. Don't be fooled. Writing and communicating as beautifully and naturally as this is a rare and wonderful thing.

Christine Morgan
Head of Radio, BBC Religion & Ethics

*

Introduction

Poetry Emotion is a multi-purpose collection of 50 original poems incorporating specific contents to cover three major areas addressing social and emotional values: the Barnabas RE Day themes, general themes encouraging social and emotional development, and related emotional skills. The resource is ideal for RE and Collective Worship at KS2/P4–7. Within the three major sections, the poems are organised under 15 topic-based chapters, and each values-based chapter offers a choice of up to four poems exploring different aspects of the theme.

The prime purpose of the material is to feature poems that address the complex issue of being a child in a 21st-century multicultural society. Within the mix there is material for special seasons of the year, such as Christmas and Easter, as well as material dealing with hard situations that children have to face at times, such as violence, death and bereavement.

The resource is designed for use at KS2/P4–7 (7–11s) in Collective Worship and RE. Each of the 15 chapters offers an introductory paragraph setting up the topic, to guide teachers and pupils alike as to how to use the poems. The poems then speak for themselves. The idea is to provide a springboard into open discussion, or a thought-provoking insert (or pause point) in an act of Collective Worship. Simple suggestions for follow-on classroom activities are included, aiming to stimulate creative writing and thinking. The suggestions are offered with an open and accessible approach, making them equally beneficial for independent readers and wider markets beyond the classroom door.

Although each section concentrates on a specific theme, it is hoped that the teacher will feel free to pick any chapter at random, without feeling bound to approach the chapters sequentially.

Please use the book as best suits the mood and requirements of the class.

*

Barnabas RE Day themes

The poems in this section reflect some of the themes explored through a Barnabas RE Day:

- Whose world?
- Who am I?
- Who is my neighbour?
- What's so special about the Bible?
- It's not fair!

A Barnabas RE Day is a full day's visit to your school to bring the Bible to life for primary-aged children through a range of the creative arts. It provides a flexible, enjoyable and educational experience, which will unpack stories and themes from the Bible alongside contemporary life illustrations.

If you would like to make an enquiry about a possible booking, please telephone the Barnabas team administrator on 01865 319704 (Mon–Fri, 9.00am–5.30pm) or send an email to enquiries@brf.org.uk.

*

Whose world?

Teacher's notes

This opening chapter of three poems addresses the themes of the planet's welfare and a child's 'deep thoughts' about it. The poems are written to stimulate observation, a sense of stewardship and even ownership in children, underlining the fact that this 'home' is theirs and they can exercise a responsibility over their immediate environment.

A group discussion could arise along the lines of what we can do in response to the challenges made by the poems.

I would suggest that this group discovery exercise could begin with the third poem, 'A shark of many names'—asking, 'How many different species of shark are there?' (answer: in excess of 370) and then going on to list some of them and discover some fascinating facts about this complex creature. For example, *National Geographic* research reveals that only about a dozen shark species are dangerous to humans, in particular the great white, the tiger and the bull. The exercise should also emphasise how some species (the hammerhead and porbeagle), as highlighted by the International Union for Conservation of Nature, are threatened with extinction through overfishing.

You may even wish to consider 'adopting a shark' as a school, as a response to personal and collective ownership of the 'Whose world?' theme. The Shark Trust (www.sharktrust.org) runs such a scheme through its conservation and research projects in British and American waters.

Family likeness

The sky is a wandering screensaver,
the mashed potato clouds—a moving queue.
The sea is a puzzle of mixed feelings;
it roars, rears up, calms down, then welcomes you.

The jungle is an orchestra of secrets,
with bass note growls and fast percussive snorts.
The moon is a glitter-ball of memory
recalling days of dancing astronauts.

And all are neither one thing nor the other,
the sky beams blue, the sea regrets its feuds.
The jungle sleeps; the moon forgets it's lonely...
like us, they are wild worls of changing moods.

• • • * • • •

Because the Earth...

Because of swarms of satellites
there's not much space in space.
Because of the cruel hunter's trap
a tiger cannot chase.

Because an oil well cracked then spewed
the ocean's thick with loss,
the dark glue of the surface
jails the frantic albatross.

Because we're careless at the beach
our plastic bag will sail,
mistaken for a jellyfish
to choke the minke whale.

The Earth asks, 'Where's the otter gone
whose mansion was the sea?'
She weeps for slaughtered forests
and names each fallen tree.

What if the Earth gave up the ghost,
rubbed out by greed and waste?

Too late for us to realise...
the Earth can't be replaced.

• • • ✳ • • •

A shark of many names

There's one that is a lemon
another is a nurse
another is a leopard
and two that are much worse...

This duo (one called hammerhead
the other's known as bull),
like you, are often hungry
and can't tell when they're full

The scarce mosaic gulper,
the megamouth, the frill,
the weasel and the bramble,
the sharpnose sevengill

This census of the waters
a roll call of the deep
and sharks that rest—don't really,
eyes open, not asleep

The Caribbean lantern
the angel of Taiwan
and then there is the wobbegong...
who doesn't know he's one

• • • ✳ • • •

*

Who am I?

Teacher's notes

The first poem, 'Preferences', is a list of some favourite things, including objects and places. For a writing exercise in class, ask the children to list some of their preferences—some of their favourite things. The list doesn't have to rhyme but, if it does, that will be an achievement. Whatever the outcome, at the end give yourselves 10 out of 10 and have some pretend fudge! (The first line of this poem was inspired by seeing a child on the London Underground reading one book about tanks and one about angels simultaneously.)

The tone and theme of the chapter seeks to affirm the child's individuality, even though, as tackled in the third poem, 'In the genes', we are all products of our lineage and will manifest family likeness in some aspects of our behaviour. The fourth poem, 'Exclusive collection of me', comes from my observation of conducting poetry workshops with children classed as Special Needs, where affirmation must always be a constant.

Preferences

I like tanks and angels
spaghetti hoops and Mars
sparrows taking dust baths
stick insects in jars

I like prunes and bus stops
pneumatic drills and trowels
caves and fudge and castles
icicles and owls

I like baby rhinos
fog, an empty train
liquorice and yawning
the cooling August rain

I like tinned tomatoes
elastic bands, cartoons
harmonicas and deckchairs
the screeching of baboons

I like cranes on building sites
carousels with swings
the Leaning Tower of Pisa...

I like listing things

• • • ✱ • • •

I've got to look right

I've got to look right
I've got to look right
I'm ten years old
and I've got look right
right trainers, walk tall
in spite of me height
I'll be left on me own
if I don't look right

I've got to act right
I've got to act right
move smooth and swagger
I've got to act right
gangsta rap behaviour
though I'm puny, small and slight
they'll diss me and dismiss me
if I don't act right

I've got to seem right
I've got to seem right
right mobile phone and ring tone
I've got to seem right
but I've told no one
that I've bookmarked a pottery website
best not reveal your hobbies
when you've got to seem right

I've got to sound right
I've got to sound right
'wass up?' 'I'm chillin'
I've got to sound right
but I sound like Joe Pasquale
instead of Barry White
it's a challenge for a hoody
if you don't sound right

But I want to look wrong
I want to look wrong
and ditch me urban uniform
I want to look wrong
go to school tomorrow
in a beret and sarong
a key stage fashion talking point
I want to look wrong

I want to be me
I want to be me
like a bee trapped in a jam jar
I want to buzz free
in the evening have me breakfast
in the morning eat me tea
but me mates would bait and slate me
if I turned up as me

So I've got to look right
I've got to look right
I'm ten years old
and I've got to look right
right trainers, walk tall
in spite of me height…

I'll be left on me own
I'll be left on me own
I'll be left on me own…
if I don't look right

• • • ✳ • • •

In the genes

I am apparently like my grandad,
that's what my mother tells me…
but I haven't got a coat that's too big for me,
or embarrassing trousers, or old skin,
or gravy blob spots on the back of my hands.
I don't fall asleep on buses,
or take the dog for a walk
and come back smelling of beer.

I don't swear at traffic wardens,
or remember stuff that's not in any order,
or trump on the sofa and then say 'That wasn't me,
that was Queen Victoria'… every time!

I am apparently like my grandad.
My mother says I've got his eyes…
but I don't squint at the traffic lights
and argue that I only need glasses for reading.
I don't have a rabble of ginger-grey hairs in my ears,
or make a kerfuffle about self-service scanners
at the supermarket, and moan about
all that bleeping driving you mad.

I don't go to something called regimental dinners
then come home afterwards
and sit being boisterous and still... at the same time.
I am apparently like my grandad,
and because of him I know what rabble and kerfuffle
means...
and boisterous.
But I don't know what happens at regimental dinners,
is everybody still?

I am apparently like my grandad...
but I've never been in a war,
or say little poems quietly to myself,
sometimes crying as I say them

*'Belfast, Derry and Coleraine,
those were the days we can't explain.
Enniskillen, Crossmaglen,
those were the days of former men.'*

I am apparently like my grandad,
both brave and scared at the same time...
so my mother says.

• • • ✱ • • •

Exclusive collection of me

I am hugely-much-full of spectacular
and active with hyper-hooray
I am taken-for-granted miraculous
like the Tardis and midsummer's day

I am so unexpected unusual
like a giant you've invited to tea
I am brimming inventive, original,
I'm an exclusive collection of me

So because of all this I am classified
and given my very own chair
as my words splutter out all disorderly
I am special needs... present elsewhere.

• • • **✳** • • •

*

Who is my neighbour?

Teacher's notes

The poems in this chapter incorporate both a local ('Mr Harris') and a global ('I made it to five') approach to the subject, aiming to begin, perhaps, the process of citizenship in the young reader.

The first poem, 'I made it to five', came about through my work for the Canadian-based children's charity World Vision, as I became familiar with their many outreach projects in the developing world. Their 'Advocacy in Action' programme states starkly and effectively, 'Five years is not a child's lifetime', and is a challenge to be proactive in the preventable campaign against infant mortality through diseases such as TB and HIV/AIDS (the 'big, important letters' referred to in the child's inner monologue).

A class exercise for this chapter could entail asking the very simple question, 'Who is my neighbour?' Having established the basics—'the person next door' as in the imaginary neighbour 'Mr Harris', and the real 'displaced person' who's just come to the school—the exercise, ideally, should then expand to embrace the global perspective.

The writing element should be an imaginative one, recording what sort of place the child in 'I made it to five' lives in, and what the class thinks and feels about someone, not far from their age, struggling with illness and not even having a school to go to because of poverty. It is, in effect, a 'what do we take for granted?' question and exercise.

I made it to five

I made it to five—isn't that good?
I made it to five
and, because six is a long way away,
today… I am a bright bee on a broad orchid
nuzzling the colour-swarm of morning.
Today, I am for ever now.

My blood, which keeps me buzzing,
has sick *things* in it.
Like an unwell ocean
my blood is sinking.
These *things* have very long names…
and big, important letters
to shorten their long names,
which is what they're doing to me.

Me isn't very long—just two letters—
and not big or important,
so how long will me be?

I made it to five—isn't that good?
In spite of the floods
the village needs water,
but water that's tidy and clean,
and not angry… and not sinking;
water and blood would be my best friends
if we weren't all sinking.

Today, I am having big thoughts
because I made it to five.
Today, I am for ever now
but for ever isn't very long
because of the big, important letters…

Today, I am a bright bee…
running out of flowers.

• • • ✻ • • •

Mr Harris

Mr Harris lives next door
in a house of cats.
I think it rains every day in there
because when you walk past
you can smell the damp.

Mr Harris used to have a mouldy green fence
at the front but it fell down
and now it lies there like driftwood.

Mr Harris used to go to sea
to Africa and South America.
Perhaps he was a pirate
because in his back garden
there's a big wooden chest (that's mouldy too)
and some stone statues of birds, a pelican, an osprey…
and a rusty oven
and a sundial
and a stale piano.
I think he must have brought all of these treasures home
and then forgot about them.

Some nights I hear him through the walls
hammering and drilling.
Maybe he's building a cabin
or a crow's nest
from where he'll look for new lands
nowhere near here
which is where he used to live,
on the ocean…
and not like now… on his own.

Some people think Mr Harris is very odd
and that his house is a disgrace.
But what do you expect?
He's very old, and there being
no retirement homes for old pirates,
he makes do with his own ramshackle one.

• • • ✳ • • •

Displaced person

There's a new boy in school, he sits next to me,
I've been asked to look after him too.
Make certain he's in the right classroom,
make sure he's not in the wrong queue
for lunch and assembly and break time.
He's quiet and he's nervous and small,
he got lost on his way to the playground,
I found him in tears in the hall.

He seems to be bothered by most things
and finds writing in English so hard.
He much prefers football to lessons,
he's jumpy and always on guard.
The name of my new friend is Tariq,
he's come all the way from Iraq.
His parents don't have the right visa,
I'm afraid that they might send him back.

• • • ✱ • • •

*

What's so special about the Bible?

Teacher's notes

The novelist Jeanette Winterson observes that the archaic language of the King James Bible, for her, is 'rich and problematic' but it is a text 'where the words themselves move us away from too much literalness towards an opening of the mind'.

There are, of course, more modern, accessible translations of the Old and New Testaments, but the poems in this chapter are not about which version of the Bible the ideas spring from. Rather, they are an attempt at an opening of the mind for first-time readers.

The poems, as such, stress the adventure element of the Bible and the universal stories that run through it. 'More than a good read?' is a cribsheet, pick-and-mix poem where the stories of Goliath the felled giant, the exodus of the Israelites from Egypt, and the resurrection of Christ are introduced.

'Nativity epic' is a new twist on the old 'tea-towel shepherds' nativity play. There may not be a group discussion or writing exercise for this chapter, as the subject matter is immense, but the poems can simply be used as an introduction to the great fund of adventure stories within the Bible's pages.

More than a good read?

Let's start off with a story
about a strong man with long hair
who sadly came a cropper—
and there's more! It's all in there

with its tale of talking donkeys
and fables hugely weird.
There are miracles concerning
how the disappeared appeared.

There are epics in which tyrants
get well and truly bashed,
and a fee-fi-fo-fum giant
who ends up pebble-dashed.

There are grudges and predictions
and stairs up to the sky.
There are desert walks to freedom
watched by the camel's eye.

There are contrasts, visions, legends:
Mary's kiss, The Holy Grail.
There's also 'inter-active'
in the belly of a whale.

There is courage as a shepherd
sees off a prowling bear.
There are tales of magic cities
where there's peace. It's all in there…

Nativity epic

I was such a brilliant donkey
in our school nativity play
with glitter, cardboard ears
and loud and honking bray

I practised that for hours
in spite of aching jaw
I lived the part completely
and slept at night on straw

I 'work-shopped' with Amelia
who's now got sunken cheeks.
She's such a 'method' camel
that she hasn't drunk for weeks

and Gary, brave with 'improv'
in mad, gorilla suit,
the unacknowledged fourth wise man
who ate his gift of fruit

Miss Simpson, our director,
is very 'cutting edge'.
Instead of tea-towel shepherds
we had twins called 'Ron and Reg'

They had a sword fight with the angel
who really went to town,
until our pale head teacher
then brought the curtain down

But the action just continued
when a screaming Christmas fairy
had her wand bent, and what's more
Ron and Reg got thumped by Mary

The script was ripped up by the head,
one governor went wild,
asking, why was Widow Twankey
worshipping the child?

Miss Simpson's now on sick leave
but getting better, so I hear.
She was really inspirational
with one fabulous idea:

at the end of our nativity,
she said everyone should kneel
for, just like the original,
our baby—he was real.

• • • ✳ • • •

Esther's first impressions

Well, there aren't any pictures
apart from the ones you make in your head.
Some of the stories are interesting
but the names are often quite difficult to say.
I haven't read that many
but my favourite so far is about Esther...
because that's my name.
Esther was a queen
who saved her people from a very bad man.
I don't really understand it all.
I might if it was a film
but I always like it
when people are saved...
I like those stories the best.
I was told that the Bible's got lots of stories
where people are saved.

*

It's not fair!

Teacher's notes

The poems that follow are variations on the theme of inequity and the aftershock of the realisation that life isn't fair.

'Book ends' is about the consequences of a government's policy and the effect it has on, in this case, learning and literacy, especially in financially disadvantaged areas. The second poem is fairly self-explanatory, concentrating on how the kind of unfairness described brings persistent, unresolved grief, while 'Turned out nice again' offers an imaginative reaction to perceived unfairness.

This chapter offers a potentially useful group writing exercise in which the children are invited to list 'loss' and 'profit' columns on the subject of 'It's not fair'. I've used this exercise before in schools and found it to be very much open-ended—which may or may not bring its own conclusions.

In the 'loss' column, encourage the children to express all the unfair things in life (this could be a very long list). Turning to the 'profit' column, the challenge is 'How can we make the "unfair" fair?' The answers to this second part of the exercise may surprise you.

Book ends

There aren't no books in our house,
on our shelves exactly none.
We do have an aquarium,
the telly's always on.

So, I'm going to the library
to learn to proper spell
whilst reading books on kissing fish
and coral reefs as well.

On our shelves we have ornaments
and I'm reading about those,
especially the unicorn
whom no one really knows.

I'm reading about weapons,
the sling, the exocet.
We don't have no computer
which means no internet...

And neither does the library
but that doesn't bother me.
Today I learnt what reading is...
a new word: 'jamboree'.

I'm learning about all sorts
like how tall the Redwood grows.
But there'll soon be no more reading
'cos the library's got to close.

It's 'cutting costs' (or something)…
will the government agree
that to help me with my reading,
I take the library home with me?

• • • ✳ • • •

It's not fair that...

… Lucy's chair is empty

It's not fair that the bus driver didn't see her
It's not fair that we're all crying in the dining hall
It's not fair that I now know what an undertaker does
It's not fair that coffins come in such small sizes
It's not fair that Lucy's dog can't find her
It's not fair that some grown-ups don't know what to say
It's not fair that Lucy's mum is always at the doctor's
It's not fair I'm frightened of traffic
It's not fair that I keep saying 'it's not fair'
It's not fair that I don't know how long 'not fair' lasts

• • • ✳ • • •

Turned out nice again...

It's not very fair is not fair,
it's not very fair at all.
It's not very fair that I broke my arm
falling off our backyard wall.

How did I come to be there
and what brought this about?
Through chasing next door's tabby cat
who chews birds and spits them out.

It's not very fair is not fair,
it always hurts my heart
to go behind our wheelie bin
and find a chaffinch pulled apart.

It's not very fair is not fair,
I was really at a loss;
I threw a jug of water…
now the postman's wet and cross.

It's not very fair is not fair,
it's a battle of the wits.
I enticed the cat into our house
with milk and biccy bits.

Now it's all very fair that the cat's fur
conceals a warning bell,
the gentle ringing round his neck
means the birds hear him as well.

You can change the ways of not fair,
turn not fair things around,
the cat is curled up in the sun
and the birds are safe and sound.

It's all very fair when the world's fair
but it's sometimes not at all…
this truth that I discovered
falling off our backyard wall.

• • • ✱ • • •

*

General themes

When children are encouraged to develop respect and responsibility within a well-ordered environment, they are provided with opportunities for reflection about attitudes, choices, emotions and feelings.

The poems in this section are designed to help children develop skills such as understanding another's point of view, working in a group, sticking at things when they get difficult, resolving conflict and managing worries. These themes build on the whole-school ethos through initiatives such as circle time or buddy schemes, the teaching of personal, social and health education, and the citizenship curriculum.

*

Getting on and falling out

Teacher's notes

In a way, the heading for this chapter follows on from 'It's not fair', as the first poem, 'Child benefits', explores one of the reasons why 'falling out' sometimes happens (the children being the victims of imposed circumstances).

'Zoo trip' is about mishearing and misunderstanding, and is a personal plea to accommodate the imaginative child who wants to get on and participate, but in their own way. The final poem will, I hope, resonate with both teachers and parents—the inevitabilities of the 'Friendship merry-go-round'.

One group discussion could be along the lines of the basis of friendship: why do we choose, for a season or even longer, to be best friends with someone, and what are our feelings when the friendship goes wrong? This could turn into a writing exercise (unless you feel it is better to stick to oral discussion) in which the children express their feelings about times when the emotional covenant between 'wee best pals' is broken.

Child benefits

We used to hold hands at tap and ballet
She came to my first party when I was four
We played together every single day
But Kylie's not my best friend any more

Her bedroom has a TV and a laptop
A Harry Potter poster on the door
And sleepovers were such a special treat
Why's Kylie not my best friend any more?

My dad has lost his job and can't find work
He says he doesn't know just 'what's in store'…
Is that the pound shop where my mum now goes?
And Kylie's not my best friend any more

I've learnt new words: 'embarrassed' and 'ashamed'
We can't afford the things we had before
Like laptops, ballet, tap and Alton Towers,
Now Kylie's not my best friend any more

• • • ✳ • • •

Zoo trip

'Describe to me the chimpanzee'
Mrs Taylor said.
But I was just half-listening,
wrote something else instead.
'The chip pansy
is a small, fried flower.
It's purple
but don't chew it.
It also comes in yellow—
I don't know who first grew it'...
Mrs Taylor kept me in after school.

• • • ✱ • • •

Friendship
merry-go-round

Anthony was my best friend;
generally, I quite like Jane.
Ben and me once had a fight,
Liam's 'bezzie mates' with Wayne.

Joshua is such a laugh.
Lee's not good at fitting in.
Hannah's good at getting on,
apart from getting on with Lynn.

Ben and me are now alright,
Sanjeev's best pals with Lee.
But everything has gone all strange,
now Anthony won't speak to me.

I think I'll try to sort it out
with Hannah, Lynn and Anthony
by making everyone see sense,
they all must be best friends with me…

I don't know why that didn't work
and really I'm not fond of Jane.

Now Liam's pals with Joshua,
and I'm best friends with Wayne.

Going for goals!

Teacher's notes

These poems are about objectives, both personal and imaginative—not separate but more a juxtaposition of both states.

'Missing miracle' is a 'why?' question. Having presented a BBC Radio 4 programme called *Questions, Questions* for several years, I see first-hand, through listeners' questions, how we carry this creative desire to know why and how things can and can't be, throughout our lives.

'I'm a girl with a tool set...' is about a girl I know who is fascinated by such questing. She wants to know how things work, so 'possibility science' and the beyond-the-bounds-of-credibility of 'Doctor Who' is, for her, a playground of practical imagination.

However, underpinning all this is the most necessary and ambitious application of all—the best goal to aim for—as described in the last verse of 'Not half'.

These poems will touch on dreams and hopes—some realistic, others perhaps 'a work in progress' needing refinement. However, 'why?' and 'how?' and 'what for?' are foundations for the very simple writing and discussion exercise posed by the question, 'What are your hopes?' with the follow-up, 'How do you think you can go about achieving those hopes?' Again, this exercise is not meant to be conclusive but, rather, the beginning of the practical consideration of 'Going for goals'.

Missing miracle

Monkeys choose bananas
then do a forward roll.
And on the lawn stand pyramids
constructed by a mole.

Amazingly, chameleons
can change to emerald green
but I've never seen an elephant
upon a trampoline.

Otters design water-chutes
by sliding down the rocks.
Packs of dogs get nowhere near
the airborne flying fox.

Nature boasts its royalty...
a bee that is a queen.
So why's there not an elephant
upon a trampoline?

It could be done... an elephant
upon a trampoline...

I'd like to join an elephant
upon a trampoline...

Then we could bounce together
upon a trampoline.

I'm a girl with a tool set...

I'm a girl with a tool set
and I'm making things
with my little ratchet screwdriver,
I'm making things
I built a hutch for my rabbit,
fixed the doorbell—now it rings!
I'm a girl with a tool set
and I'm mending things

I'm a girl with a tool set,
I'm designing things.
In the shed with my dad,
I'm constructing things
with a set square and a saw
and lots of work-bench things
I'm a girl with a tool set
and I'm planning things

I'm a girl with a tool set,
I'm creating things,
drinking pop with my dad...
we're discussing things,
sorting screws and rawlplugs
(did you know some nuts have wings?)
I'm a girl with a tool set
and I'm making things

I'm a girl with a tool set
and I'm mending things...
Just because I'm a girl
doesn't mean I can't build things...
I'm a girl with a tool set
and I'm making things

• • • ✱ • • •

Not half

half awake
half asleep
half a tic
on half a sheep

half a chance
half-raised scarves
half-time talk
game of two halves

half of two
is half a pair
half a cake
so half not there

one and one half,
numeric law,
is half plus half
plus half once more

half a ghost
half appears
flag half-mast
half cried tears

half fare half price
in half an hour,
petals dropping
half a flower

half remembered
is half true
but *all* my heart
I give to you

• • • ✱ • • •

*

New beginnings

Teacher's notes

I was in a new-build school in the north of England. The gleaming construction was imaginative both in design and use of space, a stimulating environment in which to learn. There were motivational signs strategically placed outside classrooms, quotes from writers and world figures, as well as deftly worded, positive admonishments as in the first line of 'First day at school—reading the signs'. The poem virtually wrote itself after I'd seen that.

So the opening poem and 'School dinner queue' are about the plain white paper of fresh starts. 'Season of light' continues that theme but is counter-intuitive, finding a new beginning in the long, dark stretch of winter, when the darkness of the season suggests the opposite of light.

There is no obvious exercise to accompany this chapter, apart from my suggestion of reading the poems in the given order, then asking the children which poems they like best and why. This may lead to a discussion about what are the children's favourite new beginnings (school holidays, going to new places and so on). Being in an orderly environment, for some children, is a new beginning: it's a constant reminder to me of how school, for them, fulfils their need for structure, a place where they can 'begin again' each day.

First day at school—reading the signs

Thank you for not bringing chewing gum into school
Thank you for walking on the left-hand side
Thank you for queuing quietly outside the classroom
Thank you for not running in the corridor...
... or hopping in the library
... or skateboarding in assembly
Thank you for not abseiling through the head teacher's
window
or painting the school piano pink
Thank you for not addressing each dinner lady as Nigella
Thank you for not using the drainpipes as giant
peashooters,
didgeridoos, or a hiding place for pythons
Thank you for not making space in your haversacks
for the Himalayas, buffalos or hurricanes
Thank you for not telling your mums and dads that this
school
doesn't believe in Parents' Evenings so there's no need
for them to turn up
Thank you for understanding that this school has tried
to think of everything
Thank you for reading the signs

• • • ✱ • • •

School dinner queue

Today I will
love cabbage
look forward to broccoli
get excited by cauliflower
scoff down parsnips
ask for a double helping of green beans
choose lentils
say 'yum yum' to courgettes
happily munch raw carrots
prefer turnips
exclaim 'How brilliant—seaweed!'
hope for beetroot
pile my plate with lettuce…

Just thinking about this
is making me hungry…

'Erm… please can I have a lot of chips
and a big slice of pizza…
and a radish… No thanks, just the one.'

• • • ✱ • • •

Season of light

And the clocks have gone back as they do
as a barn owl begins to pursue
a dusk-concealed, undergrowth shrew—
but this is the season of light.

When the spectre of mist blurs the streets
and our bedtime means often cold sheets,
in the dark fields a lonely sheep bleats—
yet this is the season of light.

And all is made pure by this beam,
the sea sparkles, leafless trees gleam
and sea gulls glint, glorious sheen—
praise this brief season of light.

So lights out, it's turned half past ten,
and this day was the length of a wren,
and these nights last again and again—
still, this is the season of light.

· · · ✳ · · ·

*

Saying 'no' to bullying

Teacher's notes

This is a subject I wish I didn't have to cover. However, the poems attempt to deal with some aspects of the emotionally paralysing subject of bullying.

The second poem, 'Stop it!', is the voice of the child, rationalising and trying to come up with a strategy to withstand his or her persecutor. 'Drawing things out' was a testimony told to me by an adult, although the body language, facial expressions and almost whispered speech were those of the inner, still fearful child. I just made the lines rhyme.

From my perspective, there is no cure-all solution to bullying, but 'Best not to' seeks to advise and suggest ways of confronting one of these injustices of childhood.

I would not, because of the complexity of this issue, suggest any exercise arising from this subject. Rather, I leave any follow-up to the discretion of the teacher. From my many years of having the privilege of going into schools, however, I can say that reading the poems could stir up issues, revelations and confessions, so it is best to be prepared for that possibility.

Drawing things out

Kelly says that I can't draw
she also says I'm slow
she calls me really horrid names
she says I'll never grow.

She teases me and seizes me
and pinches me as well
and sometimes when she's very bad
she's waiting at the bell.

I don't know why she picks on me,
Sarah's just as small.
I wonder if it's all because
my picture's on the wall.

Miss Jarvis put it up there—
that's a saucer, that's a cup…
and a sink with magic bubbles,
it's a wizard washing up.

Kelly says it's rubbish
and stupid and no good.
Miss Jarvis doesn't know this.
Do you think she should?

When I leave school I hope to be
an artist who is tall.
Will people still be nasty
if my picture's on the wall?
… that's my picture on the wall.

• • • ✳ • • •

Stop it!

'Give me my ball back...
it's not yours
and stop pushing me...
you shouldn't do that to anyone
because it makes you not a nice person.

And stop jumping up and down on snails
and bending branches down
because you'll break them,
trees can't fight back or say "stop it!"

And don't snatch my sweets off me
and then drop the empty packet on the floor...
just STOP IT! STOP IT! STOP IT!'
... that's what I'm going to say to him
... that's what I hope I'm going to say to him
... what I want to say to him...

• • • ✱ • • •

Best not to

Best not to have hidden
best not to have cried
best not to be ruled
by the panic inside.

Best not to give in
to the taunts of the pack,
or turn tail for home
the longest way back.

Best not to feel hounded
or frozen afraid...
but... best be a castle
that none dare invade.

Where lions pace the drawbridge
all loyal to you,
best be a fortress
where dread never grew.

For all the best heroes
started off scared... so
far better... grow courage...
it's a warrior word.

• • • ✱ • • •

*

Good to be me

Teacher's notes

The tone of this chapter shifts from feeling diminished and of no account, to announcing yourself, your uniqueness, 'your only you', by way of the rainbow-painted megaphone of the imagination.

The final poem, 'I take me for granted', came about when I was commissioned through the radio production company Loftus Audio, for BBC Radio 4, when we made the series *Wide Awake at Bedtime*. This involved accompanying children to various museums around Britain and recording their responses on location to such weighty subjects as space, science and the human body. (My thanks to producers Jo Coombs and Eve Streeter for their invaluable part in that process.)

This final poem, I would suggest, could be the springboard to another 'fascinating facts' group discovery session. For example, in one of the programmes, we visited Eureka!, the National Children's Museum in Halifax, West Yorkshire, where we discovered the weight of bones and water in the body. (We also played the pinball game of tracing how food works its way through the body—always a winner, especially with boys.)

Full of myself

I'm a big, bright circus, me,
all red and yellow
and loud, gold trumpets.
I'm the clown's trousers
you can't help but notice.

My Auntie Sharon says that I'm
'full of myself'
which is a daft thing to say really
because if I was full of someone else…
then I wouldn't be me, would I?
I'd be just pretending to be me,
I'd be an imposter,
or that great, new word I've just discovered:
a counterfeit—which has got nothing to do
with refurbishing shops.

I'm my own dictionary, I am,
never lost for words,
although Auntie Sharon says that happens
to old people,
they lose words…
When you're full of yourself
in the right way
you notice lots and lots
and you end up
having too many ideas at once.
I'm the spider's giggle, me,
scuttling up behind you.
What do you mean, 'Spiders don't giggle'?
How do you know?
Go on, prove they don't…
There I go again…
being full of myself.

• • • ✳ • • •

Friend in need

Imagine, now, my dinosaur
who's largely huge
and full of roar,
with feelings cave and chasm deep
who weeps and trembles in his sleep.

So, don't suppose my dinosaur
is as he looks,
for at his core
are secrets of a billion years,
he's told me these between his tears.

How curious my dinosaur...
immense, intense,
but inside, sore,
who easily can snap a tree...
yet counts on someone small like me.

• • • ✱ • • •

I take me for granted

I take me for granted,
my cortex, my skin,
a membrane of mystery
that's holding me in.

My archway of eyebrows
my tongue and my ears
my speckles of freckles
my colour, my tears.

My veins like a river,
my liver—a pearl,
my chromosomes name me
a boy or a girl.

My heart, a rose engine,
both fragile and strong,
my chorus of blood cells
a cherry-red song.

My lungs, a ribbed grotto
as confirmed by X-ray
unparalleled fortune
of my DNA.

I take me for granted.
What exactly's a gland?
Such things I don't know...
like the back of my hand.

*

Changes

Teacher's notes

Drawing on the old saying, 'Words are how you hear them', the following three poems focus on the development of personal responsibility.

The selection features 'A few words of advice' and the changes they bring; 'Days of grey', showing how a major change in domestic circumstances can bring about a shutdown in a child's development; and 'Class project: rediscovering our past', describing the rapid post-war transformation that history has brought to bear on children. This poem was prompted by my visit to the Museum of London, where I'd gone to interview the curator about 19th-century child poverty. As I was waiting, I overheard a group of schoolchildren chattering about an exhibition they'd seen, which turned into a child reportage poem.

One group discussion and writing exercise that could arise from these poems is about the number of changes the children experience in a day, from arriving at school through to going home, and how those changes affect their moods, such as rushing for lunch, dawdling back to class afterwards and so on. This exercise could be expanded to include the changes the children go through outside school, especially at home.

A few words of advice

Beware of matches
they cause fire
Beware of sharp things
like barbed wire
Beware of growling
motor cars
Beware of tigers
outside bars

Beware the river's
undertow
Beware of never
saying 'No'
Beware of diving
in Loch Ness
Beware of always
saying 'Yes'

Beware of clogging
up the sink
Beware—the word means, also,
… 'think'.

• • • ✱ • • •

Days of grey

These are my grey socks
I wear them every day
along with my grey underpants
I live a life of grey

I've had them on a month.
You must think they're not clean
I'll wear them two more weeks
Then—into the machine

I don't feel safe with change
I'd rather stay with grey
I've only been like this
since my father moved away

· · · ✳ · · ·

Class project: rediscovering our past

Yesterday we went to a museum
and looked at old photographs of children.
Children were in black and white then.
They were in a war so they had
to be sent off to farms and places,
they got on special trains
and tried not to cry.

When the war surrendered
the children went to the seaside
and the boys sometimes wore school caps
and the girls had dresses with bows at the back
and some children had round glasses
and smiled a lot
and their teeth were funny.

They played in the street until it was nearly dark
and the girls skipped because there were no cars.
Then they went indoors and had small food...
bread and jam and not much else
and they sat cross-legged in front of a fire and read
books.

And everyone was poor
in these photographs
but they weren't somehow
and they were children like us
but they weren't somehow...
In the future, will there be a photograph
of our class in the museum?

• • • ✱ • • •

*

Emotional skills

The poems in this section are designed to help teachers to promote positive behaviour for learning and enhance the quality of relationships between staff, children and other members of the community. The programme aims to support teachers to transform their school or build on its strengths.

*

Self-awareness

Teacher's notes

The following four poems give the inner voice its say, from the fantastical 'Thought patterns' to the functioning desolation of 'I miss you, Miss'.

The eagled-eyed reader will have noticed how the female teacher crops up throughout the poems in this book. During my formative years in primary school, my teachers were female, ranging from the terrifyingly stern (we are in the late 1950s here) to the encouraging and comforting. Other than parents (if they're present and active in the child's life), it goes without saying that the teacher is the main role model, confessional and counsellor in many children's lives, on hand to guide the child through the often painful stages of self-awareness.

Again, this chapter may not lend itself to an obvious exercise. Rather, it's a case of reading some or all of the poems and seeing what response, if any, is sparked. You know your charges best. They are on their 'Automatic journey', and will not need, in this case, to be cluttered up too much with a 'must-do exercise'.

Thought patterns

Clip clop slip slop
marmite macaroon
marzipan chapati
school-free afternoon

Sand dune odd tune
kangaroos that sing
Frisbee played with cowpats
now there's a messy thing

Snug mug cream jug
unexpected fleas
dogs with tail extensions
mice refusing cheese

Tock tick up hic
trousers inside out
butterflies that whistle…
what's all that about?

Tap tip flap flip
killer whales that shrink
you can call this nonsense…
but this is what I think

• • • * • • •

Automatic journey

My head is very busy
it stops and starts all day
a traffic jam of feelings
a clogged-up motorway

But then the gridlock eases
through a juggernaut of thoughts
with wheel-spins of emotion
a top gear of all sorts

that revs a clutch of worries
on a lonely road of fears
that's shortly overtaken
by a zoom of big ideas…

And even when I'm sleeping
my head is fast alight
a complicated satnav
in the outside lane of night

• • • ✳ • • •

Centre of attention

I love to be the centre of attention,
it's something that comes naturally to me.
I can act and dance and even play the bagpipes,
do great impressions, even water-ski.

My chosen place is centre of attention,
a Facebook hero to my many fans.
In my own world, I'm the centre of attention,
a celebrity-in-waiting making plans.

It's only right I'm centre of attention,
I never get on anybody's nerves.
My magic tricks are brilliant, so's my cooking,
likewise, my haircut, jokes and tennis serves.

There's a time though when I'm centre of attention
my star potential falls a little flat...
in my house it seems everyone's a critic
because today I'm being shouted at.

• • • ✱ • • •

I miss you, Miss

I miss you, Miss,
I'm all amiss
it's awful that you're ill.
I miss you more than missing most,
I miss you, so until
your health gets hot-soup better
with the best recovery
I'll miss you, Miss, and one thing more,
I hope you're missing me.

• • • ✳ • • •

*

Managing feelings

Teacher's notes

The poems in this chapter address the 'managing of feelings' in all their complex manifestations.

'Squirmy birthday to me...' is the voice of a child being put on the spot and obviously not enjoying it, protesting against this celebratory imposition, however well-meant.

'Troubled sleeper' presents the teddy bear as a metaphor for incidents that bring about, among other things, broken sleep patterns, while the poem 'Benny' could be a useful catalyst (continuing from the 'It's not fair!' chapter) for a group discussion or writing exercise about managing feelings—what to do with them, how to express them and so on. I've found that children are willing to express their responses to the bewildering debris of life, but at their own pace and in their own way.

Squirmy birthday to me...

(To the tune of 'Happy birthday')

Squirmy birthday to me,
please don't sing me this song,
it makes me embarrassed
and it goes on too long.

Squirmy birthday to me,
how I wish you would stop.
Though I must sound ungrateful,
it could well start a strop.

Squirmy birthday to me,
I'm now cross as can be,
all because of a tune that
draws attention to me.

Squirmy birthday to me,
it's not how it should be,
and the cake's full of currants,
this is all misery.

Squirmy birthday to me,
I'm so shy, can't you see?
And everyone's staring
at the upset that's me.

Squirmy birthday to me,
I'm so sensitive, too,
that when it's your birthday
I won't sing this to you.

• • • ✱ • • •

Floor space

I like looking down at the floor
because it helps me think.

The kitchen floor is good for this
with its dog hair,
and crusty spots of spilt custard
that are like
yellow coins that stick
to the soles of slippers.
And when I'm asked 'What are you looking at?'
I say 'Nothing.'
Then I go outside, crouch down
and watch Formula One ants
racing across the patio
and having a pit stop under the barbecue.

I once said this out loud
but was told 'not to be so silly'.
That's why I say 'Nothing' to most things now
and carry on looking at the floor.

The floor is my space,
it helps me say nothing,
so I don't have to explain anything
especially if I'm going to be told it's silly
and not useful somehow.
Looking down at the floor helped me think all this.

What to do now?

What to do now?
Too cold to play out,
it's Boxing Day morning
and no one's about.

The house full of sleeping,
I'm sprawled on the floor.
The dog's by the fridge
pawing the door.

What to do now?
The presents weren't bad…
nothing I needed
which is all a bit sad.

I got some gift tokens
and various games but…
I wanted a dragon,
a real one with flames.

What to do now?
My dragon's not here…
start counting the days
and hope for next year?

What to do now?
This day is so slow…
I'll imagine his breath
now melting the snow.

Benny

I said goodbye to Benny
Mum took him to the vet
I preferred him to my brother
He was much more than a pet

He was golden and quite muddy
a hero and a friend
He was funny and he nuzzled
Why did Benny have to end?

He'd run off chasing squirrels
and shake his favourite toy
It was a squeaking alligator…
Mum said Benny was 'all joy'

His run was like a gallop
on his daily charge about
I gave him Mint Imperials
which he crunched and then spat out

His breath was not that pleasant
but neither is my gran's
Benny barked at magpies
Me and Benny had such plans

He'd never been to Bournemouth
he'd never had ice cream
And what was Benny seeing
when Benny used to dream?

Benny got a tumour
I hugged his head and cried
I'm feeling numb and angry
now that Benny's died…

Well, he has… but also hasn't
He's a racing memory…
Wherever Benny went to
Benny's still with me

• • • ✱ • • •

Troubled sleeper

Afraid of the dark
and quiet with dread
my teddy is hiding
far under the bed

Sweet songs don't soothe him
nor chocolate-spread bread
I've switched on the light
but night scares his head

I leave my soft pillow
and join him instead
to comfort with kisses
'sleep now, frightened Ted'

· · · ✳ · · ·

*

Motivation

Teacher's notes

The poems in this chapter deal with the theme of 'motivation'—the inner drive that can help form principles for living. The first poem, 'Some words', uses contrast in a word-play context to explore and arrive at a motivational 'core value', as revealed in the last line of the poem. This poem, in particular, is a good agent for a writing exercise. Invite the children to make two lists, one of 'positive' words (such as sun, playing, balloon, jelly) and the other of perceived 'negative' words (such as sad, lonely, sprouts, rain). Then ask the children, on their own or in small groups, to take some of their positive and negative words (such as sun/rain) and try a simile exercise (as in the poem).

For example:

Some words are orange like sun
Some words bring shivers like rain

To conclude, perhaps reconvene the class and ask which is their 'best word in the world' and why. (A core value may be revealed through this process.)

Some words

Some words get dizzy like roundabout
some words look oval like egg
some words attract us like giggling
some words are desperate like beg

Some words are distant like Paraguay
some words are dangerous like sharp
some words are borrowed like mezzanine
some words like rivers… like carp

Some words cause trouble like territory
some words disquiet us like ghost
some words taste gorgeous like edible
some words smell golden like toast

Some words intrigue us like natterjack
some words alarm us like clock
some words are fluent like languages
some words exclude us like lock

Some words excite us like holiday
some words so lonely like glove
some words forgotten like memory
… but one word we must have is… love.

• • • ✳ • • •

High achiever

Today I was a penguin
then a pirate, and a frog,
and a flapping pterodactyl
plus a grunting water hog

A great day full of action
though yesterday was calmer
I started as a bumblebee
and ended as a llama

Yet on this we're never tested
'cos I'd definitely pass
and certainly come top
of My Imagination class!

• • • ✳ • • •

My mother smells...

My mother smells of pizza,
toast and shepherd's pie,
my mother smells of ironing
and washing almost dry.

My mother smells of hair-gel,
her cut is short and slick
and sometimes if the baby's ill
my mother smells of sick.

My mother smells of perfume
although she's getting on.
My mother smells of 'girls' night out',
she's almost forty-one!

My mother smells of safety,
is that so of other mums?
My mother smells of worry
when the debit statement comes.

My mother smells of patience,
but if I'm doing wrong
my mother smells of very cross
which doesn't last that long.

My mother smells of many things,
of chips, a duvet cover,
styling mousse, soiled bibs, and love...
these smells are all my mother.

Winner of at least 103 gold medals

I'm competing in the daydreaming Olympics
I've come first in every single race so far.
Next to come's the javelin, then triple jump
after which I'll be the Games' undoubted star.

My shot put was the furthest thrown in history,
it soared to an extraordinary height
and hit a passing bus outside the stadium
which gave the upstairs passengers a fright.

I'm outstanding at the daydreaming Olympics,
this afternoon I'm in the swimming pool.
Then tomorrow I will triumph in the steeplechase,
the best daydreaming athlete in our school.

• • • ✳ • • •

*

Social skills

Teacher's notes

For this final chapter based on 'social skills', we start with an imaginative way of keeping a teacher at school ('Kevin confesses'). Thinking back to the 'Changes' chapter, when a teacher leaves a school it's a huge change for some children, as many have told me—both children and teachers.

We then move on to avoidance and an adept use of 'social skills' to write about not doing something ('12 really important reasons for not doing my homework')—which, in this case, takes as much effort as doing the homework in the first place. And, finally, we come full circle, returning to the 'Poetry Emotion' of the book's title in 'Talking it through'.

A final exercise could be to discuss and write down which poems in the book have meant the most to the children, along with the suggestion that they might like to write a poem on the same subject as their favourite, but from their own perspective.

Kevin confesses

Yes, it was me, Miss Jenkins,
I thought you'd be glad.
I'm sorry, Miss Jenkins,
the Personal Ad
I put in the paper
has turned out not good.
I'm sorry, Miss Jenkins,
I hoped that it would.

I'm sorry, Miss Jenkins,
that you're in a rage
but how could I know
that isn't your age?
And, I can see, Miss Jenkins,
how that got your goat
'cos you're fifteen years younger
than the number I wrote.

Yet well done, Miss Jenkins,
you've had four replies.
Not one you'd describe,
though, as 'happening guys'.
They've all got beer bellies,
one plays the drums,
one collects tractors,
two live with their mums.

I'm sorry, Miss Jenkins,
I can see you're upset
that I put 'can be blonde
or attractive brunette'.
Don't cry now, Miss Jenkins,
you'll get yourself down,
your hair isn't 'mousy',
it's more 'interesting brown'.

I'm sorry, Miss Jenkins,
I won't do it again.
But can I just say
about my Uncle Len.
He's single, not ugly,
same interests as you,
'crosswords, fellwalking'.
So would Uncle Len do?

He's an ace bloke, Miss Jenkins,
doesn't smoke, drink or bet.
He's a plumber, pays VAT,
with his own maisonette.
And if you got married,
you'd stay at this school.
And I'd be your nephew,
Miss Jenkins—how cool!

• • • ✱ • • •

12 really important reasons for not doing my homework

1. I left my pet grapefruit on the bus and I can't think straight without it.
2. I had to count my collection of caterpillars, which was quite tiring.
3. My pullover was itchy.
4. I asked my mum if we could have a donkey. And she said, 'No.' And I said, 'Why?' And she said, 'Because we live in a council house and we can't keep pets'... so that put me off things.
5. 37 caterpillars is a lot to think about.
6. My brother called me 'gargle bum', which wasn't very nice.
7. It's really difficult to do homework when you're wearing gloves and a Spiderman mask.
8. I just had to write a poem which goes 'Homework is boring, it leads to snoring. I'd rather be drawing.' So I was very pleased with that.
9. I started to think, 'Why can't I choose my own subjects for homework?' And then came up with such a long list, including: designing special contact lenses for the black rhino so they can see and charge at ivory traders from behind. So, all that took me ages... but then I lost the list.
10. I drew a picture of a donkey being Spiderman.
11. I spent quite a while wondering if caterpillars also feel itchy because of their fur.
12. I'm no good at homework.

Talking it through

I'm cross, I'm cross,
I'm cross, cross, cross,
I'm cross as I can be.
I'll tell you why I'm cross
because nobody's hearing me.
I've tried to speak quite quietly,
politely and with charm
but never being listened to
sets off my cross alarm.

I'm cross, I'm cross,
I'm cross, cross, cross
I hate the noise cross makes.
My voice is sore
through shouting more—such energy it takes.
I'd like to swap the bellowing
for mellowing and hush
but what makes cross
so cross, cross, cross is being told to 'shush'.

It's got me nowhere
being so cross
and cross, cross, cross is sad.
It's caused this problem being cross,
my nickname's now 'mad lad'.
So, I'm sitting feeling not so cross
allowed to have my say
as the counsellor is helping
make the deep cross go away
… soon no more cross
well not as much
I'm crossing cross, cross out!

• • • ✳ • • •

Enjoyed

this book?

Write a review—we'd love to hear what you think.
Email: reviews@brf.org.uk

Keep up to date—receive details of our new books as they happen.
Sign up for email news and select your interest groups at:
www.brfonline.org.uk/findoutmore/

Follow us on Twitter @brfonline

By post—to receive new title information by post (UK only), complete the form below and post to: BRF Mailing Lists, 15 The Chambers, Vineyard, Abingdon, Oxfordshire, OX14 3FE

Your Details
Name _____
Address_____
_____
Town/City _____ Post Code _____
Email_____

Your Interest Groups (*Please tick as appropriate)

☐ Advent/Lent   ☐ Messy Church
☐ Bible Reading & Study   ☐ Pastoral
☐ Children's Books   ☐ Prayer & Spirituality
☐ Discipleship   ☐ Resources for Children's Church
☐ Leadership   ☐ Resources for Schools

Support your local bookshop
Ask about their new title information schemes.